# THE RUTH HELLER WORLD OF LANGUAGE

"To say that Heller has a way with words is to understate a multifaceted talent. . . . Rarely do books offer children so much to look at, listen, and learn."

*—School Library Journal*

**Behind the Mask**
A Book About Prepositions

**A Cache of Jewels**
And Other Collective Nouns

**Fantastic! Wow! And Unreal!**
A Book About Interjections and Conjunctions

**Kites Sail High**
A Book About Verbs

**Many Luscious Lollipops**
A Book About Adjectives

**Merry-Go-Round**
A Book About Nouns

**Mine, All Mine**
A Book About Pronouns

**Up, Up and Away**
A Book About Adverbs

To
Totally
Cool!
RONNIE ANN HERMAN

PUFFIN BOOKS
Published by the Penguin Group
Penguin Putnam Books for Young Readers, 345 Hudson Street, New York, New York 10014, U.S.A.
Penguin Books Ltd, 27 Wrights Lane, London W8 5TZ, England
Penguin Books Australia Ltd, Ringwood, Victoria, Australia
Penguin Books Canada Ltd, 10 Alcorn Avenue, Toronto, Ontario, Canada M4V 3B2
Penguin Books (N.Z.) Ltd, 182-190 Wairau Road, Auckland 10, New Zealand

Penguin Books Ltd, Registered Offices: Harmondsworth, Middlesex, England

First published in the United States by Grosset & Dunlap, Inc.,
a member of Penguin Putnam Books for Young Readers, 1998
Published by Puffin Books, a division of Penguin Putnam Books for Young Readers, 2000

1 3 5 7 9 10 8 6 4 2

This edition ISBN 0-698-11875-8

Printed in the United States of America

# RUTH HELLER
## WORLD OF LANGUAGE

# FANTASTIC! WOW! AND UNREAL!

## A Book About Interjections and Conjunctions

Written and illustrated by
**RUTH HELLER**

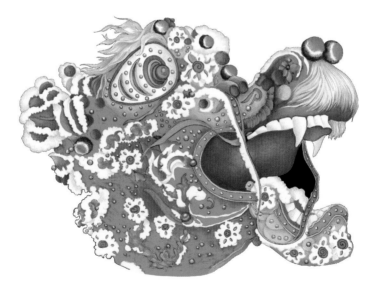

PUFFIN BOOKS

INTERJECTIONS
are words
we use
to
declare…

Good
grief!

Out
of
sight!

Holy
cow!

That's
her
hair.

They're capitalized
and punctuated,
and stand alone
when emphatically stated...

My stars!

Sakes alive!

Heavens
above!

The
owl
and
the
pussycat
fell
in
love.

A mild
INTERJECTION
requires
a
comma.

**Well,**
these are all
camels
and...

...this is a llama.

Awesome! Cool! Fantastic! Wow!

are all INTERJECTIONS that people say now.

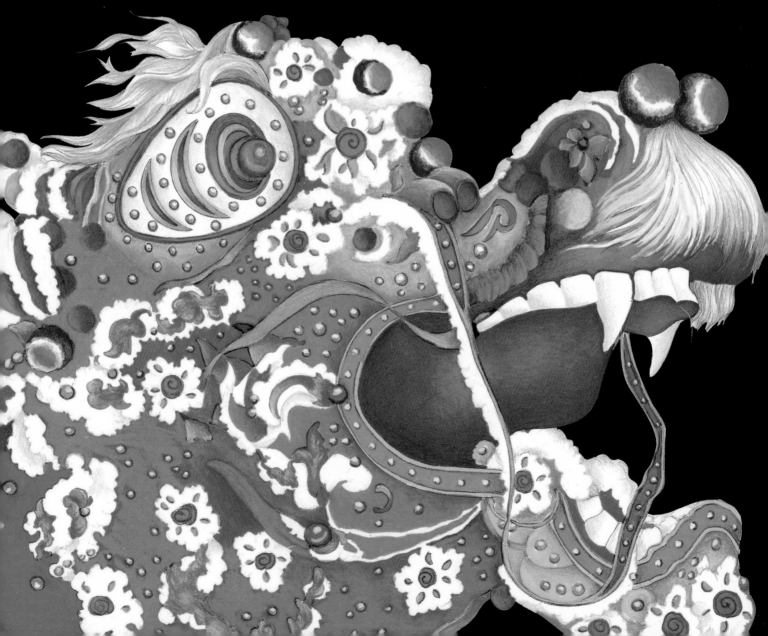

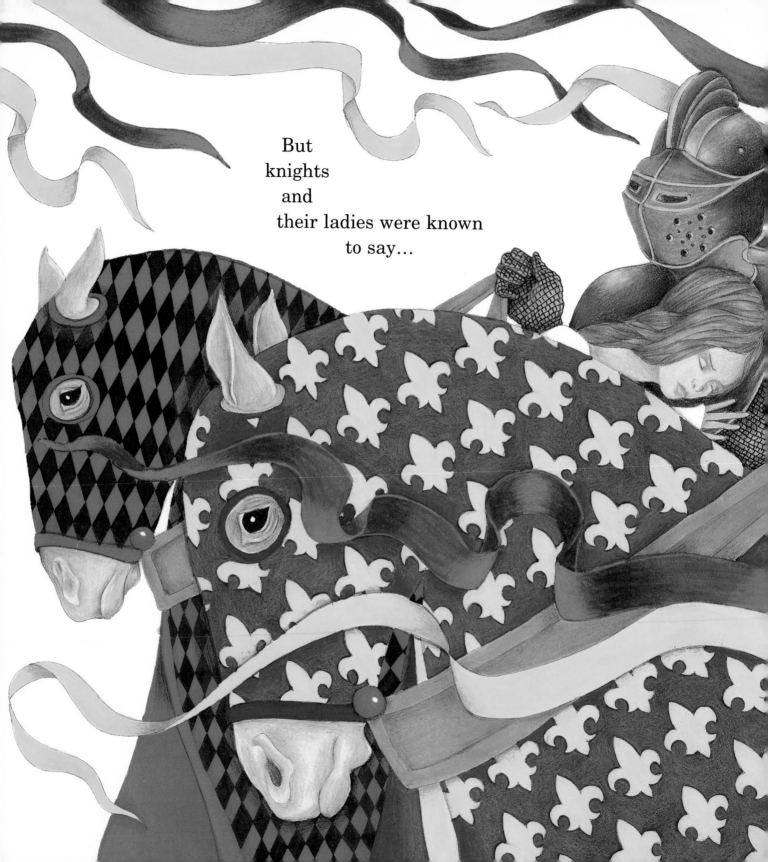

But
knights
and
their ladies were known
to say...

**Alas!
Alack!**
when
they had
a
bad day.

INTERJECTIONS
change with
the
times.

As
for
CONJUNCTIONS,
there
is
nothing
new.

•

CONJUNCTIONS
connect.
CONJUNCTIONS
are
glue.

They
join
words
together
**and**
groups
of
words,
too.

CI LXVII IL

DV XIII MV

Odd…

XV DCLXIX IC

LXXV XCV

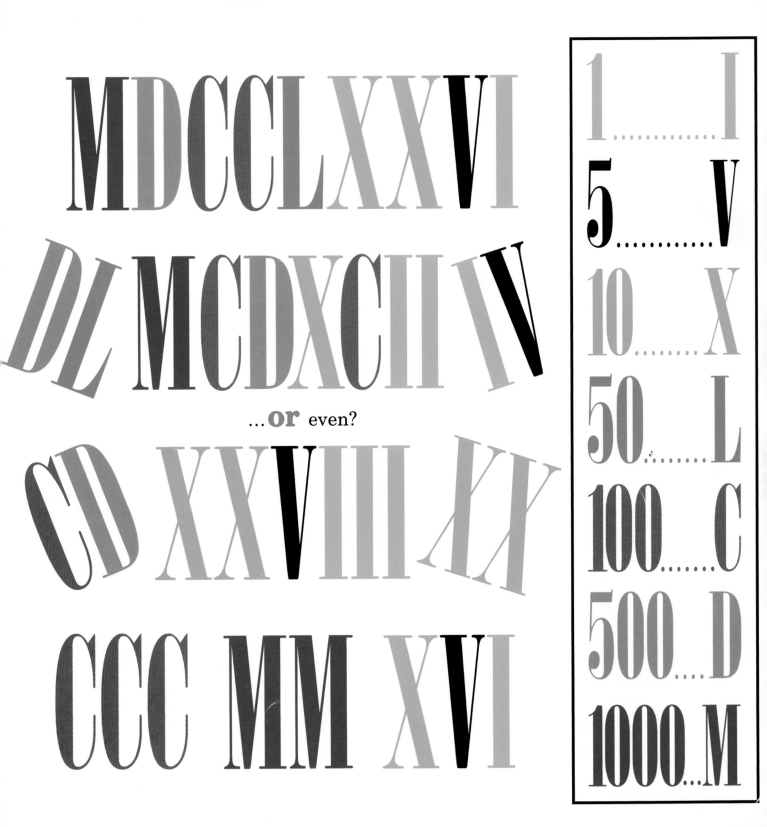

MDCCLXXVI

DL MCDXCII IV

...or even?

CD XXVIII XX

CCC MM XVI

| | |
|---|---|
| 1 | I |
| 5 | V |
| 10 | X |
| 50 | L |
| 100 | C |
| 500 | D |
| 1000 | M |

Strange,
**yet**
true.

These
sea dragons
swim
in the
ocean
blue.

**But**

...don't always believe your eyes,
**for**
no one is tallest,
**nor** anyone
smallest...

...**so**
these people are
all the same
size.

**And
or
yet
but
for
nor
so**
are very
important
CONJUNCTIONS
to know...

...and so are **if** and **because** and **although**.

**Although** this is a...

...wondrous sight, these zebras
do not look quite right,
**because**...

...they
should
be
black
and
white.

**If**
ever zebras
looked like these,
they may have had a rare disease.

Some
**CONJUNCTIONS**
travel
in
pairs.

I'm afraid of **both** tigers **and** bears.

**Neither** one **nor** the other one cares if **either** their teeth **or** the claws on their paws tear **not only** my nose **but also** my clothes and whatever they find underneath.

**When** adverbs connect,
adverbs are glue.
They behave the same way
CONJUNCTIONS do.

I have a rooster;
**furthermore**,
I've a hen;
**consequently**,
I've eggs
that will hatch; and **then**
I'll have a new rooster;
**perhaps**
a new hen,
**since**
the very
same thing
often
happens
again.

When
pronouns
connect,
pronouns
are
glue.

They behave the same
way
CONJUNCTIONS
do.

There was
an old woman
**who**
lived
in
a
shoe.

A
COMPOUND
CONJUNCTION
is
a phrase,
not a word.

As a
matter
of
fact...

...I'm sure
you
have
heard...

...another
old woman
swallowed
a bird.

**As a result**,
we think her absurd.

Each kind of CONJUNCTION behaves just like glue,
connecting words and groups of words, too.

## COORDINATING CONJUNCTIONS

and   or   but   for   nor   yet   so

## SUBORDINATING CONJUNCTIONS

although   if   than   though   unless
because   provided   whereas
whenever

## CORRELATIVE CONJUNCTIONS

both   and   either   or
neither   nor   whether   or
not only   but also
although   nevertheless

## CONJUNCTIVE ADVERBS

also  consequently  therefore  else
accordingly  hence  furthermore
then  perhaps  as

## PRONOUNS used as CONJUNCTIONS

that  who  what  whose  which

## COMPOUND CONJUNCTIONS

on the contrary   on the other hand
as a matter of fact   in the meantime
as a result   in addition   in fact
as long as   as soon as
in order to

Congratulations!
Hooray!  Hurrah!
Yippee!
Hallelujah!
Whoopee!
and
Aha!